Stri

CW00525512

Reema Sherin

@busyreadin__

Copyright © 2023 by Reema Sherin

All rights reserved.

This book or any portion thereof may not be reproduced or used in any manner whatsoever without the express written permission of the respective writer of the respective content except for the use of brief quotations in a book review.

The writer of the respective work holds sole responsibility for the originality of the content and The Write Order is not responsible in any way whatsoever.

Printed in India

ISBN: 978-93-6045-003-8

First Printing, 2023

The Write Order
A division of Nasadiya Technologies Private Ltd.
Koramangala, Bengaluru
Karnataka-560029

THE WRITE ORDER PUBLICATIONS.

www.thewriteorder.com

Edited by Ridham Bassi

Typeset by MAP Systems, Bengaluru

Book Cover designed by Sankhasubhro Nath

Publishing Consultant - Priyanka Lal

*"They didn't believe me when I told I feel too much,
so I published a book."*

Dedication

To those who were taught to bury feelings.

REALISATIONS

The little child
who grew up in a
burning home,
became the adult
who failed
to love anything that
doesn't cause a fire.

There were days when you died a little,
when your soul was trapped
in a corpse that breath,
when your smile smelled sorrow,
but seemed brighter,
your eyes drowned
yet they praised its depth.

how strange is that,
there were days
when you weren't you,
and no one noticed.

Wish I met my younger self
in that old journal,
who knitted dreams,
and placed them among the stars.

maybe,
suffocating between those pages.
'cause she hasn't made it out alive
from the chapters yet,
or wondering,
why the pages were drenched,
though I burned it long before.

How strange,
we fall for the ones
our heart craves,
only to write poems about
'why they never had
the courage to
fall for us.'

People change,
not like seasons,

but as
waves and shores,
storm and calm,
day and night,

before we even know
time has made a mistake,
after we've drifted into
the reality.

At some point,
we were so afraid of people
perceiving our
insecurities,

that we tried hard
to paint ourselves
with perfection and failed
terribly.

I always felt,
the greatest decisions in life
come unexpectedly,

like a blink, a sigh.
a midnight thought, and a teardrop.

through a regret that haunts,
and a hope that gleams.

And the hardest part of
letting someone go
isn't about filling the
voids that formed in their absence.

sometimes,
it's about finding the purpose
of every piece
they have left
in us.

Behind every person who
never know when to let go,
was that little child
who was taught to believe
that the depth of love
is measured
by tolerance.

What's more tragic
than being a soul that's born to be understanding,
never the 'understood'
labelled as someone
who is meant to be an observant,
never the 'observed'
whose tears are invisible to other eyes
where happiness screams in every possible colour.

Some of us never knew the process
of unloving someone,
even when it seems necessary,
instead,
we tend to fill ourselves with confusion,
wondering what made us cruel
enough to let them go.

We still hold onto
a few strings that knit our
memories together.
because,

all the voids that might form
by letting go of those pieces,
will never get a chance
to be filled by
anyone else.

You began to confuse
chaos and love for so long
that once you got the
chance to get out of the circle,

and never tried to gather
the courage to look back.

because this time,
you stayed long enough,
to know the difference.

Sometimes,
the people that take up
most spaces in our hearts
are the ones
who barely need a space at all.

If there's anything that stops me from pouring my
heart out to someone,
is an instinct that nobody is able to perceive how I
feel,
thus, I was always on a constant hunt to find words
to decorate every thought that I come across.
I was afraid of misinterpreting things I told,
people underestimating the values I gave to it,
along with the constant fear of being misunderstood.
maybe, that's why writers tend to find peace between
words.
because,
if there's anything that's safe to be told unapologetically,
it's only safe within those papers and poetry.
there we fossilize everything that touches our soul.
there lies every single word that failed to escape our
mouth.

Sometimes,
all I think about is how
could I miss those,
who stand right beside.

strange,
now I know why
one of the corners
in my heart is a cemetery,
made for different versions
of the same people,
who decided to disappear
and never returned.

I wasn't afraid to let it all go,
what terrifies me is the
thought of all those things
I held onto,
falling into the
wrong place.

Wish I could tell my younger self,
people aren't supposed to be
pleasant, always.

so that she wasn't locked
in a castle she built
out of nightmares,
being too afraid of letting
the wrong one
rescuing her.

We all have a chapter
which we refuse to read out loud,

something,
that's bookmarked
with the darkest shades we know.
yet,
goes unnoticed by people.

a page,
that changed
the whole course of our life,
but we kept turning.

a scent,
lies within the papers
that's neither pleasant
nor bitter.

it lies within the corner
of our hearts,
that we would probably
take to our graves.

Sometimes,
I look at people
and realise how their souls are stained
with colours I don't even know.

whose heart had gone
to the most unsafe places,
enduring enough to get forever
lost in deep trenches
with no return.

now tell me,
why is 'heartless'
an unpleasant word?

Someone asked,
'does time really heal wounds?'
how could I explain,
that time conceal it all,
with every possible colour.
only for those who are willing
to let it paint.

and I met people,
who were broken enough
to form a
masterpiece.

Strange,
the way I decided to blend in
with the oceans,
knowing I wouldn't survive.
only because someone told,
that I'll be rescued.

and here I am,
to let them know about
the way I gasped for air,
until I learned to swim
on my own.

I knew it wasn't love
when I realised
all those things I finally
learned to let go,
never attempted a return.

I knew it wasn't healing
when I was asked
to go through
the darkest phases
only to fix the ones,
that weren't broken by me.

Out of all the chaos,
what wrench my heart the most
is the fear of losing
my own pieces when I finally
learn to let go.

time may heal wounds,
but the scars remind me
of everything that befell.
and I fear,
maybe one day,
I would love those
scars too.

Not every pain
is measured by tears.
so he hid it within
the walls of his heart,
building a potential demon.
Only because someone told,

'crying makes you less
of a man!'

It's strange,
pretending that the storm
hadn't taken away everything
even when our bruised hands
screamed,
the way we held onto something,
trying not to blend into the chaos.

but we failed sometimes,
only to miss a few colours
of the rainbow
that came after.

Once you were forced
to gulp down words,
because you were too afraid,
if it'd be pleasant enough.

until your voice began to drown,
gasping to feel found,
unable to reach the surface.
yet they ask,
'why are you drenched all the time?'

I haven't figured out
what's more tough yet,
trying to fit into their idea of perfection
or convincing myself that
perfection is nothing more
than an idea.

I don't think I ever missed anyone
as much I have missed myself, at times.

from that little one
who used to look up at the sky
and wonder how come the earth's round.
the teenager,
who struggled to fit into different occasions
to a confused adult,
who made the dumbest decisions.

I didn't know how to associate myself with 'me'
while rewinding all those things
that made me feel alive.
and that's the reason why I began to knit others
and let them know how badly I missed those days.

I kept those memories closer to me,
even if the people left
because my heart learned to crave for
feelings it made during those moments,
rather than the faces that were in it.

How many times,
did we let them
walk over our hearts,
and wondered why is it too
fragile to love someone new?

We fed ourselves with colours,
hoping it'd resemble art.

for those who couldn't love us
for the way we are.
so I asked,
'would you still love me,
even if I run out of all the
shades you love?'

that was the day
I began to embrace
every canvas that was left
unpainted.

I have a terrible habit
of welcoming ghosts
who have no intention
of haunting me.

-*overthinkers*

There came a point,
when we ran out of colours
to console our thoughts
that kept turning colourblind.

then we met people who felt like night,
who endure
mystery and wore stars.
and in the end,
we learned to blend ourselves in the dark
to be a nyctophile.

They mourned
over the words that were held back.
but none knew
about the beauty of the silence
that sprout over the chaos to provide
shade.

don't you think,
there are some words
that are better off
when left unsaid?

Strings

How beautiful,
the way we decorated
the walls of our hearts
by knitting those best memories,
which cuddled us to sleep,

until someone burned them down one day,
suffocating us with its ashes
during midnights.

We all carry a story,
buried deep within the corners
of our hearts,
waiting to be watered and sprouted.
but somehow,
we learned to replant it in corners
where none had the access.

only because we knew
it wouldn't be pleasant enough
when it bloomed.

Isn't it scary,
some people simply
come into our lives,
and uproot all those
sorrows hidden in our secret fields,

then we barely found
a new place to bury it all,
so we start to plant it in
corners of the ones,
who finally began to fall
in love with us.

Have your heart ever wrenched
to see that
they are still here
in the same story,
yet different chapters,
pretending as a character
you never met.

I think that the most powerful version
of loving someone
is about learning to embrace their flaws.
that's when we begin to go against all the
'ideal' conventions that were once accepted.

we neither conceal their imperfections nor complain.
because when thinking of those people,
the little pieces that they're insecure about,
might be the portions that are customised
to fit into our idea of perfection

and that's rare.

Wish I could meet my younger self,
not to tell her how we
messed a few things up,
but to assure her that
a few mistakes
could take us
to the right place.

It took me years to realise
that 'home' could be anywhere
under the sky,

where your heart
doesn't have to crave
for the peace you always needed.

We weren't in love with the people,
we were in love with
the way they made us feel,
laughter that was offered,
and the sorrows they shared.

like a mirror,
we saw our own reflections on them,
which we struggled to find
elsewhere.

if it's only the people that mattered,
'love' would have ended
once they're gone,
and the feelings might have
faded in their absence.

Not all memories are stored in our hearts.
some are hidden in those old perfume bottles,
the little plant pot your mom loved,
half-torn photograph,
scribblings in that old notebook,
broken crayons
and the monsoon rains.

because,
once our hearts get filled
with everything that we barely need,
we look upon things
that are capable of activating our dormant memories,
in search of the will to live all over again.

How humble are we?

Home isn't a place,
it never was.

rather,
it's the million pieces of memories
knit together along with those
unshared feelings.
and we knit people on the last string,
to form a bundle
that resemble us.

I wonder,
maybe my soul craves
for the calmness I found in
the dark,
which every sunshine failed
to offer.

because I must be used to where
I have been,
rather than where I should be.

Why I keep failing to realise,
that the ones I am holding on
for so long never deserved
a chance to stay.

sometimes,
that's the reason why
my heart runs
to the darkest corners and
keep coming back with
all the things,
that I decided to let go.

When I look at you,
my heart wrenches,
realising you wept all night
wondering why your thoughts
felt too heavy to carry inside your head.

wish I could tell you,
it's because
your soul screams in colours,
unknown to those
who asked you to
wear it like a crown.

I unravelled people,
who are afraid of flowers,
due to the thorns they carry.

then I met those,
who grow gardens
in summers,
for that one bouquet of hope,
to carry all the way
till the end.

Once I saw myself
opening the door of 'past',
and welcoming ghosts
that pushed me off the cliff
into an endless pit.

then I looked around
to see them running off to corners,
because I came up with
untamed demons
that live inside me.

Don't you think,
moving on is like running
away.
we wouldn't figure out
where we're heading and
eventually pick up a pace.

exhausting,
yet we realise,
looking back is way harder,
than slowing down.

There's a phase between
holding on
and
letting go.

where our memories stay dormant,
we tried to get out
of that zone and gave up,
just because it holds the last string
that knit our hearts together.

How odd is it to wait,
hoping someone might heal us
someday.

little did we know,
all these times
we were labelling ourselves as helpless,
only to mourn over a scar,
assuming it as a wound
that bleeds.

No burden is as heavy as
mourning over the past,

which should have been left
there to rot.
but we carry it all along,
sniff,
and rant about the
scent we hate.

Don't you think,
nightmares actually occur when
we're wide awake,

and demons aren't around us,
they are within.

Some of us are cursed with the ability
to conceal ourselves so well,
afraid of those
who couldn't love us
if we finally get out those shells.
maybe that's where we failed
to express who we really are.
that's the most terrible mistake we've made so far.

Perhaps,
our greatest flaw is
settling for the thought of
how it should be,
rather than
how it could have been.

I think,
not every writer has gone through enough to write
about something that people could relate to.
some of them simply know the tragedy of
leaving words behind for the sake of peace.

maybe,
that's why you tend to see yourself somewhere
between those lines and fall in love with them.
because out of all these confusions, there is someone
out there,
who is able to express what you've been feeling all
this time.

oblivion of who you are and which language you're
able to perceive,
writers are able to bring you closer to a small fictional
space
filled with people who let out their fragile hearts run
free,
just like you.

And if that isn't a beautiful scenario, I don't know what
is.

Tell me,
the tragedy of seeking peace
in people who only taught you
to embrace
chaos.

The truth is,
sometimes all I want is someone
who'd remind me that
no matter how terribly I fail,
as long as I breath,
some things are simply worth a try.

People never realise how simple things they've done or told,
leaves a lifetime impact on others.

I still wear that bracelet my friend gifted when I was sixteen.
Those cursive lines in my school autograph still take me back to the good days.
I wasn't into books until someone told me about her favourite line.
I used to smell my dad's old empty perfume bottle whenever I miss home.
A show suggested by a random stranger shaped the way I used to think.

certain simple things I assume to be erased by time,
never got a chance to leave.
Maybe the people won't,
but some feelings, gestures, and memories
that are imprinted on our lives grow
over time and circumstances.

REMINDERS

I hope you forgive yourself,
for living in fields where the
flowers haven't bloomed in years,
I hope you forgive them,
for asking you to believe
that your heart isn't made to
embrace spring.

Strings

May the stars remind us
why admiring the dark
was so

necessary.

How often we forget that,
no matter how hard we try to fill each chapter
with the right ink,
once turning those pages,
we all are villains
in someone else's story

and that's alright.

Sometimes,
walking away is the most powerful version
of acceptance.

because,
it takes all of one's self to silently let go
of that one last string,
that no longer finds a reason to hold on.
yet,
reserving a space
for a return that isn't promised.

It suffocated you once,
but that doesn't mean
you'll have to spend
an entire lifetime
trying to hold breath,
to know how grateful you are
for needing the air you deserve.

-victimising

I hope you wouldn't let someone,
who make you
feel guilty
for embracing the sunshine,
when you're built
to burn along with
the sun.

you aren't *too much* for the right one.

Behind every person you meet,
who was cursed with a cold heart,
is the one who once burned
the things they loved,
to let others gleam.

finally
to get stranded
in places where the
light haven't entered
in years.

How terrifying,
when you come to know,
everything that is capable
of being loved unconditionally,
is bound by the concept of
being fiercely unloved.

Remember that child,
who was afraid to cry out loud,
afraid of those voices that might escape,
since he'd be blamed for creating chaos around.
the girl, who wrote things down, hoping it'd die along
with her.
that one who tried to blend in with everyone.
If not, he wouldn't be accepted.
the one who felt lonely,
yet surrounded by loving people.

who used to mentally prepare himself to go 'home',
or labelled as emotionless.
only to end up as someone who feels too much.
the one who carried oceans in heart,
but never got to complain about the storms that came
once in a while.
he has got an urge to pour that heart out to somebody,
but hides it as silent weeps under the ceiling fan in
sleepless midnights.
the one who dreamt of calmness,
because she has fought wars inside that no one has
ever tried to address.

and look how far that little child has come.

There are certain feelings,
you could neither name nor explain,
like the spectrum of colours
unknown to certain eyes,
your heart is absorbing it like art.
but here you are,
apologising for feeling too much.

We tried to run away from nightmares,
which often,
made us deprived of the rest
we were longing for.
but then I know,

what if it wasn't about
silencing the demons that scared us,
but to dance along with them until
they're tired enough
to let you go?

One day,
you'll realise that all the things
that you ran away from,
never really left.
it was you,
who begin to see things
through a different perspective.

it was you,
who moulded your mind
to let things go and accept.
all that you assumed as a loss,
is still lying somewhere in a corner,
waiting for the arrival
of something new
to be forgotten.

it was all about how you've been,
rather than what
you've gone through.

I hope your heart only
bleed for those,
who aren't afraid of
the stain.

I hope your soul only
bloom for those,
who aren't afraid of
the thorns.

How often we fail as a human to realise that every
person
that is glued to our lives has a unique perception
about life.
maybe, the whole concept of perception
isn't all about the half full/empty glass.
Because for some people,
it's all about the existence of an object that simply
satisfies their thirst.
Likewise, most times we unknowingly hurt ourselves,
simply demanding everyone around to make us feel
'seen'.
oblivion of their view about the scenario or us.

if we could understand the chaos that churns someone
from inside,
the world would be a little bit free from heartbreaks
that aren't capable of mending.
perhaps,
if hadn't let our eyes decide what's within a soul,
our hearts might have realised about the weight it
carries.

Just because they loved
roses too much,
doesn't mean you
have to carry the thorns
in your heart for them.

-*people pleasers*

Maybe,
those endings that we assumed
as endings,
weren't endings at all.

what if,
it's our heart turning away
from the sun for a while
only to know how peaceful
it must feel like wandering in the dark.

Have you ever thought about that person
who decides to spend their lifetime standing on the
other side of the sea,
waiting for your storm to find a shore,
the one who had the courage to stay
a bit longer on days when there is no promise of the
sunrise,
among those who only praised you for your sunny
days

and how often we forget that even the kindest souls
can get tired of understanding and not understood.

this is a reminder,
to embrace this blessing
before it goes out of sight.

Yes,
it's worth a heartbreak,
but that
doesn't mean it's worth
living with a broken heart.

I hope your heart finds home,
where your laughter echoes in
in every corridor,
where your smile is framed
on every wall,
with swings and mirrors
in every corner,

I hope you find home
in someone,
who reminds you that home
is not a place.

It took me years to realise
the way my heart wrenched,
sleepless nights,
and endless storms,
were the prices that destiny
made me pay to reveal that

all the things that run away
from me,
never deserve
a chance to be chased.

Some chapters are meant
to stay unfinished.
those stories are
either written by destiny
or a few are burned by
'time'.

all because at some point,
you ran out of the right ink.

and that's okay.

How often
we have a will to fall
for a broken person,
blaming the unhealed version of us,
reflecting on them.

but what if,
it's actually the healed version of us,
reaching out to mend it.

Remember,
just because you found
comfort in the dark once,
doesn't mean
you have to forget about the sun
for a lifetime.

-toxic relations

Sometimes I think about
how often we were lied to believe
that every pain we have gone through was supposed
to shape us.
the truth is,

not everything you have endured is
going to end so well.
some simply stays out there as a misplaced puzzle
piece,
searching for a space.
and I hope you'll learn to stop customising yourself
to let that fit in.

Isn't that strange,
to see people concealing their grief so well,
we often get the illusion
that some pains are easy to carry.

I hope you'd stop welcoming
ghosts living in the dark,
waiting to devour your soul,
only because someone
turned your lights off.

That's when you realise
what's the point of punishing
yourself again for letting the light in,
to the places that were broken
by those who never wanted
 you to see the sun?

Just because you love the ocean,
doesn't mean you have to
drown in it.

-*obsessions.*

How often do you fear about losing yourself
as much as you're afraid of
losing others?

remember,
the pieces you let go
in order to glue others into your life,
goes along with them.

Behind every person
who decided to bury
their feelings in unknown places,

was that little child
who was taught to believe
that love blooms
only when there is
enough suffering.

There are some stains,
blend into your soul
with colours you failed to name,
refusing to fade,

and you carry them
like art.

How much did we let go,
that asked to be held.

how much more are we holding on,
that demands to let go?

Sometimes,
healing isn't about
taming every demon
that devoured you once.

it's also about living with it
until you're brave enough
to release them,

at the right time,
at the right place.

How often you forget to cherish your worth
just because you were asked to settle for less than
what you deserve?
the people, things, feelings or emotions,
all because you were shaped to think that every good
ones
that's meant for you comes with a sacrifice.
the truth is—it isn't.

all the divine things that feed your soul
are written for you.
and I hope you never give others
the chance to determine the reason for your existence.
because,
'you' and your worth are the possession that only you
can carry,
not them.

I hope one day
you'll forgive yourself
for dissolving into the chaos
you made
in your head.

I hope one day
you'll stop forgiving them
for asking you to create the chaos
you never know about.

There comes a phase,
when you'll run out of places
to keep your true self hidden.

that's when you get the courage
to drown those
who made you believe
that it's a drought.

Not every story demands
an ending.

a few ones are meant to stay
unfinished.
not because of the tragedy that followed,
but of the beauty in the lines
that need to be preserved,
in spite of all the
odds.

Often,
emotions blindfold us.
and we begin to endure
everything that falls upon.

because it's easy
to spot every aura that's around,
but it takes all of ourselves to realise,
those were actually
the reflections
of our own sparkle,
from within.

Sometimes,
we become too confused
to understand the difference
between what we have
and what we deserve.
let it be people,
things or feelings.

settling for less
than what we deserve
is something
we are designed to accept unintentionally.
and that is the first building block
of every regret
we carry.

We all have times,
that wasn't worth a space in our heart,
but take up almost all the corners.
but somewhere in between,
we learned to bloom over our grief,
concealing every void
with things that made us
seem happier.

the truth is,
if people were defined
by their dark days,
the world would be a
cemetery.

I wonder why
it took me years to the realise,
it's not the people around
that are blind to see our wounds.

It's actually our hearts
that kept bleeding in colours,
unknown to those who
never went through enough,
to love us for what we have been.

Sometimes,
the things that we loved the most
become the ones we barely remember at all.
not every feeling we have carried
is meant to last a lifetime.
the wounds, scars, tears, laughs and giggles,
the things you left for good,
the ones you held on for the worst.
all those we assumed to leave a mark on our hearts,
were simply another chapter,
waiting to be turned.
maybe that's why I always felt like there's nothing
which time isn't capable of answering.

Perhaps,
if we aren't too busy to believe that,
not everything that's wished
is meant for us,
we wouldn't be ungrateful enough
to see that
everything that we believe
to be meant,
wasn't wished upon us.

You'll never know the tragedy
of silence,
until you are asked to
bury your words
in places where your voice
will never enter.

What's meant for us,
may not always
find us.

maybe,
it isn't about finding it at all.
because ensuring ourselves with
optimism in destiny is all we need

even to cross puddles
when oceans seem impossible.
somehow,
a few beliefs push us through,
though we barely made it to the end.

I hope you realise,
everything that you're trying to fix
wasn't broken by you.

Not every wound
is meant to heal.

a few stay,
only to remind us
why we bleed often.

Remember,
those wars you've lost
weren't because you don't
deserve to win.

but,
those were never
worth the
win.

Sometimes,
the things we talk about the least,
could be the ones that haunt us the most.
how often we were forced to stop letting those words
escape our mouths,
being too afraid of the vulnerability that follows.

from failed relationships to the career that wasn't
pursued,
every person you know might have something
that made them question their worth.
maybe,
if we were taught to believe that there's nothing
wrong
in letting people know that we aren't alright at times,
might have made all those possessions a little easier
to carry.

it's okay to not be defined by only better days;
it's okay if you can't master the art of pretendence.

Sometimes,
closures are disguised as,
the things they failed to notice,
the way you felt lonely around them,
the times your heart wrenched in silence,
the places you no longer feel their presence.

some closures are meant to be felt,
only by you.

It isn't love,
when you keep finding them
in all the places you lost yourself.

In the end,
what matters is not if you wanted to go ahead of somebody,
what if the whole point is whether the slow and steady pace
made you reassess every perspective
that has the capacity to view life from an angle you weren't aware of.

sometimes,
we are too busy to look upon things that life threw in-front of us,
that, if gone,
would never get a chance to be remembered.

from those unintentional mistakes to unforgettable regrets,
the journey that chose you is about which path you took,
rather than who was behind or ahead.

if that makes you the weakest among them,
then what's the point of being the strongest among all?

REMEMBRANCE

Of all wounds that refuse to heal,
your name is the one
that bleeds.

I may forgive
but I won't forget,
when you blamed me
for the chaos I did not create.

and every flower you pass through,
will be my letters to you
from the graveyard,
where you buried me
with your silence.

I still remember,
your last words were,
"how'd your heart turn cold?"
maybe I wouldn't answer,

is it because my heart
was used to the winters
you offered than the
sunny days I craved,
or was it
since I burned all my dreams,
just to keep you warm?

I never knew
why our souls
kept running away from calmness
and stayed in storms.

wish you would realise one day,
though my heart only knows
tragedy of the chaos I create,
there's still a part of it
that aches silently,
craving for the peace
of your return.

How could I show you
what spring feels like
when your heart is all
about winters.

yet,
I don't know why
I use to weep all night,
when you complain
about all those plants
I watered for our love
never got a chance to bloom.

Strings

I wouldn't dare
to have one last glimpse.
maybe,
I am afraid that you'll see
the flame in my eyes,
waiting to burn those
who pretend to console,
maybe in the next life.

don't you think,
what destiny could promise
in other lives,
that was once denied in here?

For years,
I lived in a tunnel of confusion,
wondering
how does it feel to be loved
as who I am.

and I know it wasn't you,
when you finally began
looking for me
in places I don't live
anymore.

I kept watching you,
watering the plants you loved,
in spite of the monsoons.

hoping that you'll know someday
that the roses
I planted for you,
still grow even in summers,
in that desert you
stranded me on.

After you were gone,
the same night that wore stars
delicately,
became the mystery
I couldn't endure.

I never fell out of love,
I simply fell out of those expectations
that made you look
extraordinary.

Don't you think,
we fell at the same time,
to reach somewhere together,
and meet once again.

all I remember now is,
how you slipped away somehow,
leaving me all alone
in the dark
where even the demons
are afraid to stay.

Isn't it odd,
how you remind me of spring
that never gave a chance
to other seasons.

but how could you never notice,
the flowers in my heart grew,
even across the four walls,

hoping you'd see it someday
and make me a bouquet out of it.

Wish I could tell you,
that I would even walk
to the ends of the world,
only to have one last glimpse
of your face,
maybe not to demand a return.

but to let you know,
that I deserved a better
goodbye.

Strings

I regret
falling in love with the sun
in your eyes,
knowing that it'd dry up
the oceans I carried in my heart.

and here I am,
on the verge of a drought,
trying to find a shore
where the sun never sets.

At two ends of the world,
our hearts beat together
trying to reach out.

how awful,
when one day
mine decided to sneak out,
but never found its way back
home to you.

and to me.

Even if I could absorb all the light
in the universe,
and create a spectrum of
unknown colours,

I would still choose to stay
where our shadows align.
only to misunderstand ourselves
as soulmates again.

I remember ranting
about how hard it is,
to survive the dark.

and if it wasn't you,
who made me feel like I have to burn
to be worthy of the sunshine
that I needed,

I wouldn't have to spent my days
wondering,
why I hate the sunny days too.

Once
I was offered a chance.
not to set a choice,
but to realise why things fell apart.
so that I might finally
gather the courage
to let you know,

all these time,
my heart was craving to get broken
so that you could find a way out.

You weren't made of stardust.

decades later,
I might learn to look
through a different perspective,
only to know that maybe
it's the muse in me
that made you look so
extraordinary.

it wasn't you
that kept gleaming,
it was my sparkle
that resonated
with you.

You made me realise,
everything that glittered wasn't gold.
it was the hope,
that lived inside me
disguised as a gleam.

and I will wait for you
to ask someday,
'where did we go wrong?'
only to say,
that you remind me of a place
that doesn't offer peace.

Once I tamed the demon in me,
buried it in those trenches
where plants never grew,
hiding every empty spaces
with colours I love.

I never thought it'd be you,
who would bring it back home
and blame myself
for losing
the key.

Strings

Each time you counted
the stars in my constellation,
I used to wonder,
was it your sparkle in those eyes
or my aura that reflects

now I know,
why my sky feels so empty
only to remember
that you left.

But I never knew
that I was so into you
until I hoped,
the sun would dry out the oceans
when you stepped
in a puddle.

here I am,
praying for a drought
to rescue my soul that kept
drowning in yours.

Somewhere,
between those
awkward silences and
unshared feelings,
we built a wall over our memories
to part ways.

little did I know,
it would take a lifetime
to find someone
who would love me enough
to climb over the barrier,
only to reveal that
I still crave for your presence.

He lies
somewhere between
my burned chapters.

strange,
though I drenched a few pages
yet,
he never ask for a
rescue.

I no longer carry
the weight of the nights
by letting your memories win
over my thoughts.

maybe because
somewhere between those
silent storms and cries,
my soul has finally learned
to untangle
from the labyrinth of someone,
who made me feel like
soulmates don't exist.

Maybe I don't deserve the
right to regret how
we were never meant
to make it to that verse of our story,
where we promised to stay.

but,
have your heart ever wrenched
to see that
we are still here
in the same story,
but as different chapters
waiting to get burned?

Once I got a chance,
to turn back time,
only to see us trapped in a loop.

strange,
to feel those wounds over again
and how they bled us dry.
because I reached too far,
to the point where
we said *goodbyes*.

They say,
every time you mourn over
an unkept promise,
a new star forms in the sky,
gleaming to console your soul
that suffers.

now call it poetic,
but hope you'll remember,
why I kept saying that
your eyes remind
me of a constellation.

I thought it was
the colours exploding
in my heart,
whenever I laid my eyes on you.

I felt vulnerable
once someone asked,
'maybe it isn't about
the colours after all.
what if it's your heart bleeding
by the thought of being
broken again?'

Maybe we'll meet years later
on a rainy day,
and you'll ask if I still love you.

I wouldn't let you know,
but even if all the rains
in the world drown me,
I would still choose to
refuse a sunny day
if it was you,
who offered it.

Tell me
that you shall keep me
hidden in those pages
burned by the things
you never dared to say.

because,
that's where I found
the words to paint
you,
that's where a poet
was born.

I filled my heart,
with your memories
until it burst.

now I have to spend
every midnight,
picking up all the pieces
and wondering,
if anyone would ever find out
how incapable I am
to let someone go.

Thinking of you feels like
touching a wound
that never heals,
and now I'm afraid.

what if I bleed on those
who will finally begin to
fall in love with me,
and stain their souls
with everything that I am
trying to run away from?

Once you left,
the world seemed darker,
deprived of the colours,
or maybe I turned colourblind,
unable to perceive everything
as it was.

what if
it was me,
who kept painting the world
from all those palettes you offered,
rather than the ones I had?

Maybe,
if I stop feeding the muse in me with
every promise you failed to keep,
I wouldn't be writing unsent letters to her,
asking to stop painting someone
who never know
there lived a poet
inside me.

I failed to let you know,
but the worst part about forgetting you is
I still see you in all those daffodils you loved,
the monsoon you never intended to love,
and the scribbles you made in my old journal.

perhaps,
if I have the courage to stop gazing at things the way
you loved to look at,
I wouldn't be here,
searching for your face in every crowd and place
you've never been to.

But how could I deny it?
somewhere between those days when I bookmarked
for your return and hoping to bring you back alive
from every chapter that I wrote about your loss,
I slowly began to forget how it feels to be in love.
if that's what you name healing,
I haven't healed yet.

Strings

I shall keep you
caged inside my poetry
and decorate it with every possible
word that I found.

until you starve from the memories
we never made,
deprived of sanity.

Your name will always
be pierced into my soul,
like a diamond
I failed to notice.

maybe we wouldn't share
the same ocean that I stare at
everyday.
at least,
we're under the same stars
I tell our stories about.

You Write. We Publish.

THE WRITE ORDER

To publish your own book, contact us.
We publish poetry collections, short story collections, novellas and novels.

contact@thewriteorder.com

Instagram- thewriteorder

www.facebook.com/thewriteorder

Printed in Great Britain
by Amazon

39572257R00098